It's around

Dave Boyle
Wendy Pitt

S · T · E · P

CAMBRIDGE
UNIVERSITY PRESS

Published by the Press Syndicate of the University of Cambridge
The Pitt Building, Trumpington Street, Cambridge CB2 1RP
40 West 20th Street, New York, NY 10011–4211, USA
10 Stamford Road, Oakleigh, Victoria 3166, Australia

In association with Staffordshire County Council

© Cambridge University Press 1992

First published 1992

Printed in Great Britain by Scotprint Limited, Musselburgh

Designed and produced by Gecko Limited, Bicester, Oxon.

A catalogue record for this book is available from the British Library.

ISBN 0 521 40625 0

PICTURE ACKNOWLEDGEMENTS

R.D.H.F. 16br.
Christopher Coggins 7, 15, 28.
Department of Transport 16tr.
Friends of the Earth 17bl.
Greenpeace/Hoffman/Jamestown Recycling Centre, Camden,
London 31tr.
Robert Harding Picture Library 8bl.
Images 24–25, 31b.
Kelloggs Ltd. 17tl.
Linda Proud 8, 13.
Recycling City Ltd. 27.
Reebok Ltd. 17br.
Rospa 16tl.
RSPCA 17tr.
Science Photo Library 31tl.

Picture Research by Linda Proud

NOTICE TO TEACHERS

Contents

Improving
the environment

Talking together

What is rubbish?
Where does rubbish come from?
Where can you find rubbish?

Do you find rubbish lying around your
local area?
What sort of rubbish do you find?
Could any of this rubbish be used in any
way?
How can useful rubbish be collected and
stored safely?

Is any rubbish recycled in your area?
How is it collected?
What happens to it next?

A need

Imagine your club has decided to organise a fête to raise some funds. It is to be held on the play area of a housing estate.
The local people have said they are worried that there will be a lot of litter blowing around after the fête.
You need to design and make some ways to collect the litter.

Developing your design

Planning your ideas

What sort of litter do you need to collect?

What materials would be suitable for making a litter collector?

Do you need to test the materials to find out which are most suitable?
How can you set up a fair test?

What materials can you get hold of cheaply and easily?

• D A T A   F I L E •
**Fair testing
Recycling materials**

Making structures

What makes a good structure?
Look at some of the structures around you?
Are they made from certain shapes?
How are they joined together?

You can make some prototype structures using everyday materials such as cardboard boxes, plastic bags, string and newspapers.

You may need to think about
- shape
- strength
- stability

The structure you make would need to be strong enough to hold the litter. It would also need to be stable enough to stand up to the weather conditions that you may get during the fête. Design and make some prototypes to find out the most suitable shapes for the structure.

• D A T A   F I L E •

Card and paper:
cutting
folding and strengthening
joining
Structures
stability

9

Be sure that when you are testing your structures they are given the **same** test to find out which would be most suitable.

You will need to make the test fair so that each structure is given an equal chance during the tests.

Lift weight to this line for each test

Place the bin HERE ↓

• D A T A   F I L E •
Fair testing

A need

Rubbish is unsightly and a possible health hazard.

Your headteacher would like to put some ideas to the school governors about ways of keeping the school and its surrounding area rubbish free. Everyone in the school wants a pleasant environment in which they can work.

The governors would like to see the proposals and decide which might be the best solutions.

Developing your design

Where is the rubbish?

You need to find out if and where any rubbish collects around your school.
Carry out a survey of the area and find out where rubbish containers could be placed.

Think about:

- where the paths are
- where people play
- where people stand and talk
- where the containers could be placed and not cause accidents

• DATA FILE •

Research:
data collection and display

Drawing a plan

You may need to make a plan of the school site to show where the containers could be placed.

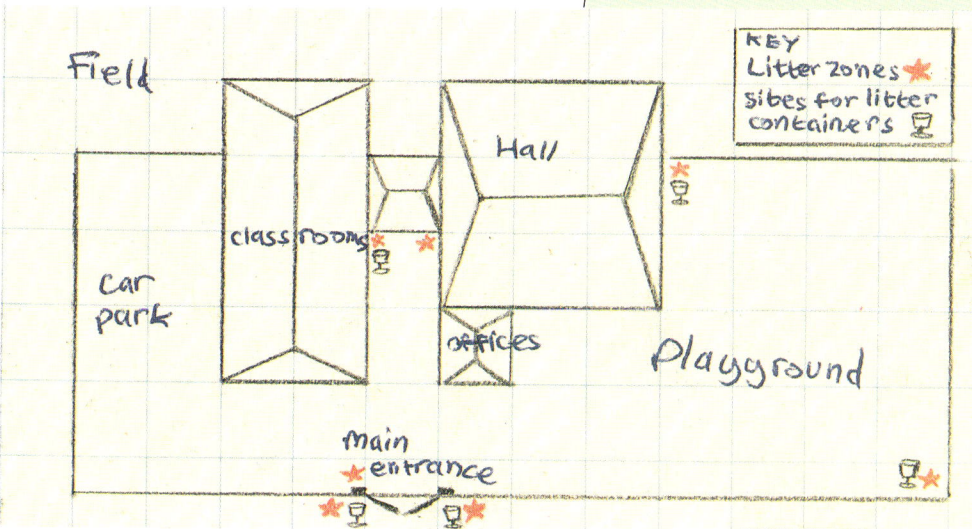

KEY
Litter zones ⭐
Sites for litter
containers 🗑

Field

Hall

classrooms

Car park

offices

Playground

main entrance

There are ready-made litter containers in parks, gardens and playgrounds. Make a collection of drawings of these containers. Would some of these containers be suitable for your school?
What do they cost to buy?
Would they be attractive around your school?

Making a model

Make a model of the school site that shows the containers in position. This model could be made from card, showing the inside and outside of the school building.

You need to think about the size of the model. You may also need to think about how much time you will have to make the model.

The governors could be shown the plan and the model to help them make their decisions.

* * * *
Litterbins in our schools

A report by class 3

* * * *

• D A T A   F I L E •

Card and paper:
cutting
folding and strengthening
joining
nets
Printing:
using potatoes
using blocks and rollers

painting roof

card roof

painting glasspaper for grass

card triangle glue on

square sectioned wood

card

card for playground and field

glue spreader and glue

litter bins

More ideas

If litter has been on the ground for a while it could be dirty and you do not want to pick it up with bare hands. Can you design something to help you to pick up litter without harming yourself?

Litter is often packaging that has been used and thrown away. There may be better ways to package items so that less litter is produced. Perhaps you can think of some ideas to discourage manufacturers from over-packaging their products.

• D A T A   F I L E •

Preparing myself
Research:
data collection and display

Posters
to inform

Using your senses...
SEEING

Use your eyes...

Talking together

Look at a collection of posters.

How easy are they to read?
Is the size and shape of the poster
eyecatching?
What colours are used?
How effective are these colours?
Have cartoons been used on the posters?
What types of lettering are used?
Where could the poster be placed to
attract attention?
What messages are the posters trying
to tell people?

Margot Says:

*Make A Date –
With Your Dentist Today*

Keeping fibre fun.

Everyday more and more people are convinced of the importance and benefit of an increase in fibre intake.

Recommending an increase in fibre consumption is easy.

To change the lifestyle and eating habits of all ages is difficult. Everyone eats for pleasure as well as sound nourishment.

While pure wheat bran is an excellent source of fibre it is not the most pleasant of foods to eat by itself!

Apart from providing fibre in palatable form at breakfast, **Kellogg's All-Bran** and **Bran Buds** lend themselves to recipe usage – not only confection but main courses too. You enjoy your meals and get the benefits of fibre while keeping fibre fun!

Have fun! Have fibre!

Send for recipe suggestions to Kellogg Company of Great Britain Limited, Stretton, Manchester M32 8RA.

I need your time and interest

I need you to take care of me for the rest of my life

RSPCA, Causeway, Horsham, West Sussex RH12 1HG. Tel: Horsham (0403) 64181

ROBOT RECYCLER

You can make your own recycling monster. Use him to store paper and other material, but not glass, for recycling.

YOU'LL NEED-

① A large cardboard box
② A smaller box for his head
③ 2 bottle tops
④ 4 cardboard packets for the arms
⑤ Old gloves or cloth for hands
⑦ felt or cloth for feet
⑧ Zip for mouth

1 Cover the boxes with plain recycled paper or old wallpaper. Use glue or wallpaper paste
2 Fix on the eyes, ears and mouth. Leave to dry.
3 Pierce 2 holes in each of the 4 packets
4 Thread string through. knot in the end
5 Fasten on the arms
6 Glue on the head
7 Fix gloves to arms. Fill with crumpled paper
8 Stick on the feet.
9 Now paint him as you like.

WHY NOT TRY YOUR OWN DESIGN?

PUMP IT UP!
Reebok

17

A need

Your school library has just been redecorated and has reopened. There are no posters around school telling everyone that the library has reopened and their favourite books are there to be read.
Can you design and make some posters for the school that advertise your favourite books and the new library?

Developing your design

Lettering ideas

Find out how to make the lettering large enough to see from a distance.
You may want to cut out letters from newspaper headlines and use those to write your message.
You may want to use felt pens to write your message.

• D A T A   F I L E •

Graphics:
lettering 1
lettering 2

A computer program could also be used to help you write the letters. You may be able to change the size of the print. Carry out some tests to find out the best size for clear print.

With so many to choose from

TYPEFACES COME IN MANY DIFFERENT FORMS

This is face is known as OCRB.

EXTRA BOLD or BLACK

A need

As part of a class topic on the environment you may want to encourage people to keep the school buildings and playgrounds tidy. A poster campaign is needed to encourage people to keep the school and surrounding area tidy.

KEEP BRITAIN TIDY!

DON'T DROP IT BIN IT!!

PUT YOUR RUBBISH IN THE BIN!

Developing your design

Planning your ideas

What kinds of posters could be made?
What shapes could the posters be?
Will they have photos, cartoons, or
collage work on them?
How could more than one
poster of the same,
design be produced?

• D A T A F I L E •

Graphics:
lettering 1
lettering 2
cartoons 1
cartoons 2
**Collage, montage
and decoupage
Production lines
Card and paper:**
mechanisms

More ideas

You could get people's attention by making a poster that has moving parts, or that people have to touch to find out the information.

You could give your poster 3-D parts to attract peoples attention to the message on the poster.

Your poster may have to be placed outside. How could you make sure that all your hard work was not washed away, if it rained?

Waste Not Want Not

Talking together

What do you throw away into your dustbins?

How much is thrown into your dustbins in a week?

How is rubbish collected and disposed of in your area?

What are the raw materials that rubbish is made from?

Is there anything that you throw away that can be used again?

How could this rubbish be used again?

How can we be encouraged to collect our household refuse for recycling?

A need

The local council would like to collect household refuse so that some of it can be recycled. They want to make people aware of the rubbish that can be recycled.
Can you suggest ways that people could sort their household refuse so that certain items could be collected for recycling?
People will also want to store these recyclable items until collection time.

Developing your design

How can households be encouraged to collect refuse that can be recycled? Householders need to be shown what can be saved for recycling. They also need to know how to collect and store these items for the council collection services.

A need

The usual council vehicle that collects refuse needs to be redesigned so that the different types of waste can be stored separately. Each vehicle needs to carry paper, plastic, glass, metals, garden refuse and waste food, textiles, and other waste that cannot be recycled.

Developing your design

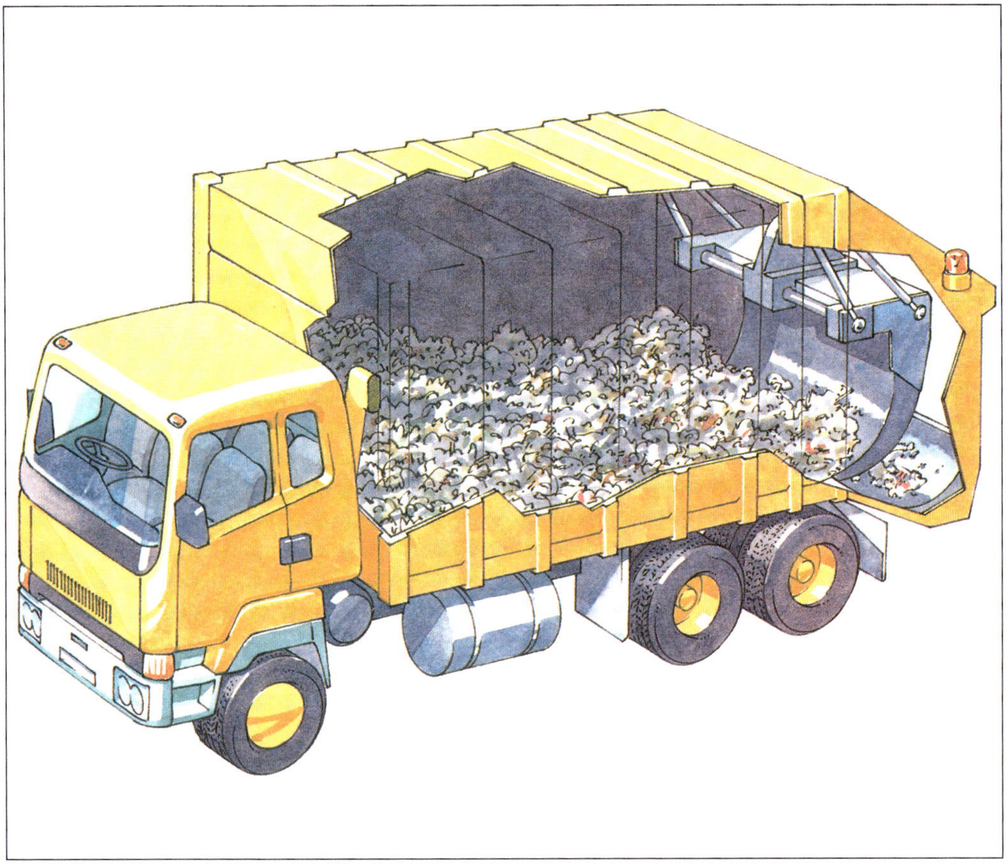

Looking at a refuse vehicle

You may be able to look at an existing refuse collection vehicle. Ask if your class can look around the vehicle when it calls at school. By looking at an existing vehicle you could think of modifications to help in the collection of recyclable materials.

• D A T A   F I L E •
Research:
data collection and display

You may be able to make some models of
your ideas. These models could be used
to make suggestions to your local council.

Someone from the council may explain to your class the way refuse is collected and disposed of in your area. You may need to write to the council to find the information you need.

Scrap glass bottles
These will be taken to a glass recycling plant, crushed and fed into a furnace.

Neighbourhood recycling centre
When people sort their rubbish and take it to centres, one truck can collect rubbish from many sites, for delivery to recycling plants.

The molten glass *is made into new bottles or jars.*

• D A T A   F I L E •

Letters and invitations

More ideas

Design a system that would help people living in blocks of flats to collect and store recyclable materials. How could the recyclable materials be collected if the flats have refuse chutes to dispose of their rubbish?

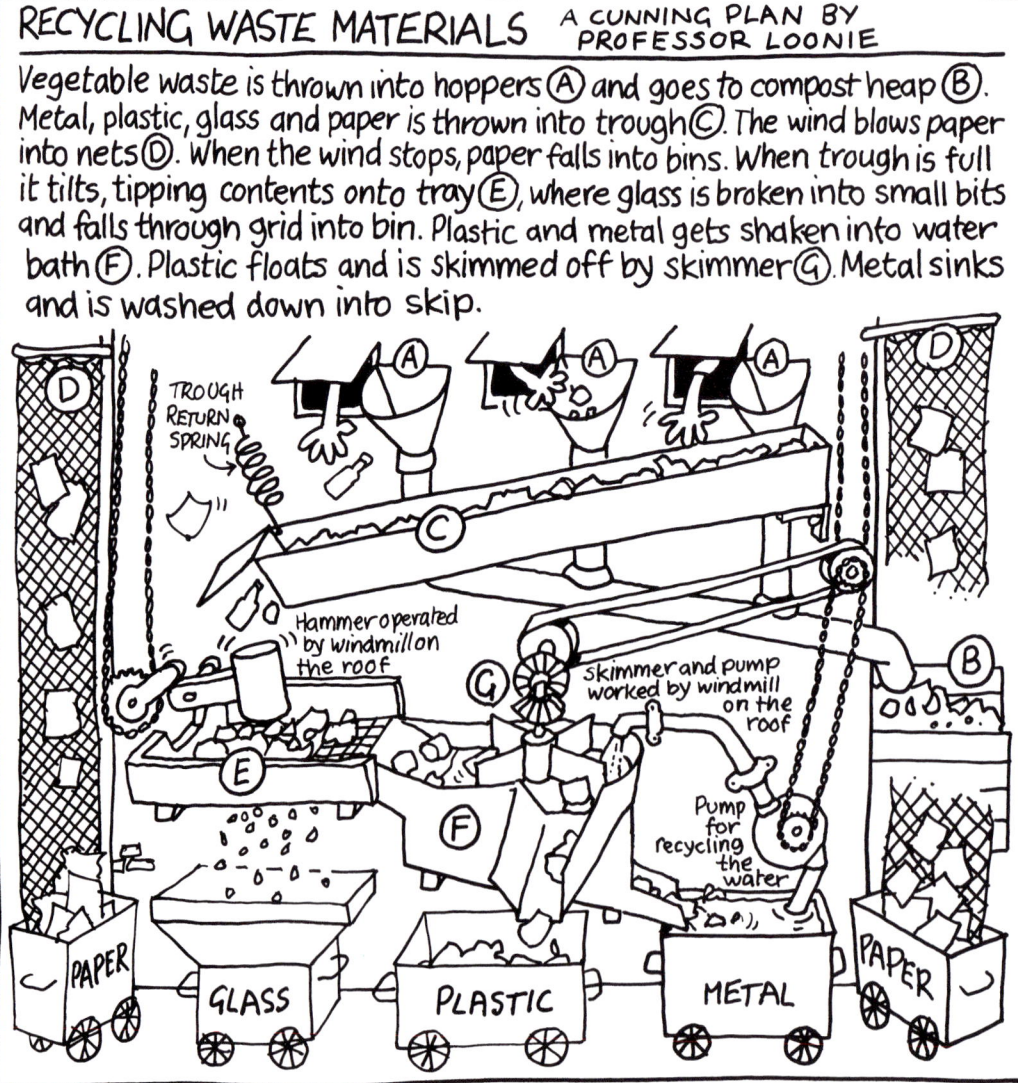

RECYCLING WASTE MATERIALS — A CUNNING PLAN BY PROFESSOR LOONIE

Vegetable waste is thrown into hoppers Ⓐ and goes to compost heap Ⓑ. Metal, plastic, glass and paper is thrown into trough Ⓒ. The wind blows paper into nets Ⓓ. When the wind stops, paper falls into bins. When trough is full it tilts, tipping contents onto tray Ⓔ, where glass is broken into small bits and falls through grid into bin. Plastic and metal gets shaken into water bath Ⓕ. Plastic floats and is skimmed off by skimmer Ⓖ. Metal sinks and is washed down into skip.

TROUGH RETURN SPRING

Hammer operated by windmill on the roof

skimmer and pump worked by windmill on the roof

Pump for recycling the water

PAPER · GLASS · PLASTIC · METAL · PAPER